The Wee Book of

THE CLYDE

Robert Jeffrey

Black & White Publishing

This book is a tribute to the skill and dedication of *The Herald* and *Evening Times* staff photographers down the years, whose work has produced one of the world's great picture archives.

First published 2002
by Black & White Publishing Ltd
99 Giles Street, Edinburgh EH6 6BZ

ISBN 1 902927 60 5

Front cover – In a classic image of the Clyde, the *Queen Mary* sweeps round the Dalmuir bend on her way to a first taste of the open sea. A flotilla of tugs help the giant in the narrow reaches of the river in 1936. To decrease the draught of the giant liner, the life-rafts were fitted at the Tail of the Bank.

Back cover – Destination: the Kyles of Bute . . . and these pensioners from Paisley, guests of the Paisley town council on the *Queen Mary II* in the early '50s, were having a ball while still in Glasgow's dockland.

Photographs on pp. 5 and 7 reproduced by kind permission of the Annan Gallery, Glasgow

A CIP catalogue record for this book is available from The British Library.

Printed and bound in Spain by Bookprint, S.L., Barcelona

INTRODUCTION

The Clyde may not feature on any list of the world's longest, fastest or widest rivers, but it is right up there among the top in any poll of the best-known rivers. 'Clyde-built' is a synonym for quality, and it takes quality people to build quality ships.

Some of the remarkable stories of the people, the river and the ships come together in this little illustrated book. There are fifty fascinating images, culled from the millions in the massive photographic archives of the *Herald, Sunday Herald* and *Evening Times* held in their Renfield Street, Glasgow HQ. These photographs originally appeared in Black and White Publishing's three-volume series *The Herald Book of the Clyde,* co-written with Ian Watson.

Life on the river and its banks has changed down the years. The clang of the yards has quietened, and the rush to the coastal resorts has weakened. But this *Wee Book of the Clyde* is something of a collective family album for a giant among rivers. It captures the moments of grandeur as the great liners take to the sea. Here, too, are revealing snapshots of the everyday life of the men – and women – who built them. And for anyone who has ever taken a trip 'doon the watter', there are pictures to bring happy memories of holidays in the great resorts in their heyday flooding back.

In the early years of the new century the Clyde is facing a new future, with hopes of massive naval orders for the remaining shipyards and talk of 'high speed' ferries from Glasgow to resorts like Rothesay and Dunoon. But here in one small book is an evocative reminder to Clydesiders of the way we were.

Robert Jeffrey

Carradale, July 2002

4

There are new plans afoot to run ferries from Glasgow down river to Greenock and on to the resorts. But a jaunt 'doon the watter' starting in the city centre is no novelty as this image, possibly from around the mid-1850s, shows. The Broomielaw waiting-room advertises refreshments, and both banks of the river are thick with a mixture of sailing vessels and steamers.

It is 1895 and three pleasure vessels, the Iona, *the* Benmore *and the* David Adamson, *prepare to sail. The cargo boats tied up ahead of them are a reminder of the river's importance as an artery for commerce.*

This view of the Broomielaw shows the many changes in the area. The dockside where the steamer lies is now the site of a casino and nearby is the shiny new Atlantic Quay building. There are plans to turn the whole area into a financial district.

10

If Broomielaw was not your jumping off point, a family could take a train from the Central Station to Gourock to catch a steamer, or maybe just spend the holiday at an Ayrshire resort, leaving from St Enoch Station. This 1915 family group has a well-heeled look to them.

No Tannoy announcements or electronic destination boards for those at Queen Street in the '30s. Here a railway official barks out train information for passengers, many no doubt waiting for transport to Helensburgh or Craigendoran – once a major terminal for Clyde steamers.

The day trip down the river was a great Glasgow institution much used by companies to foster good staff relations. It seems to have worked, judging by this happy bunch from the famous furniture store.

A famous 'shipwreck' right in the centre of town! In 1978 a very low tide caught the Carrick *out and caused her to flood. A sad episode in the life of a full-rigged ship which had sailed the world's oceans as the* City of Adelaide. *She was re-floated at her Clyde Street berth but was later taken to Irvine for restoration. Funding problems meant that she has lain there, a decaying, unglamorous hulk, for a number of years.*

18

The Caledonia, *on her last sailing of the 1969 season, passes under the almost finished Kingston Bridge. The paddle steamer was sailing into history whilst the motorway system was only just beginning to make its mark on city life.*

Just down river from the Kingston Bridge is the shiny eye-catching concert and conference venue nicknamed the 'Armadillo'. Across the river at this point today stand two of Glasgow's newest attractions – the Science Centre and the Glasgow Tower. And there are imaginative plans for a new bridge across the Clyde near this point.

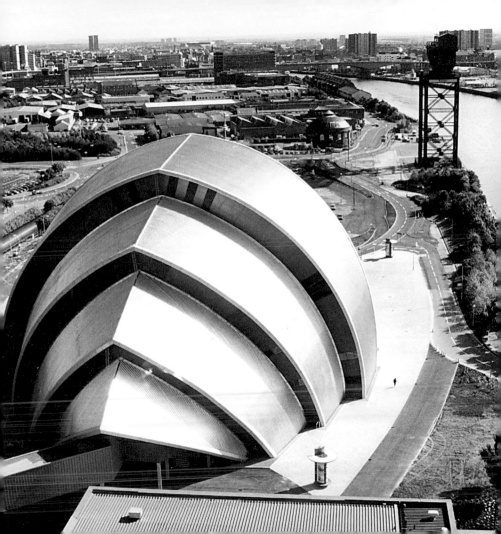

The Science Centre is located on part of the site of the 1988 Garden Festival, which kick-started much of the Glasgow renaissance in the '90s. This is what the Garden Festival site looked like in its heyday.

The tiny passenger ferries – often mainly used to take workers to and from the bustling yards on both banks of the river – used to be an attractive feature of the Clyde. But one by one they stopped running. This was the scene in January 1966 when Ferry No. 7 *completed its last journey. The skipper seems to bring a touch of the* Vital Spark *to a sad day.*

The Kingston Bridge and the Clyde tunnel in the '60s also diluted the need for passenger ferries. The tunnel was a complex project that meant the workers entered and left by compression chambers. Later there were accusations that the procedures had been inadequate and workers had suffered bone necrosis as a result. This was how it looked when under construction.

*The Clyde docker was a legendary figure who worked in
all weathers, often without protective clothing other than
the ubiquitous bunnet. This lot in the '50s enjoy a break
round the brazier. In cold weather the 'pieces' were
heated on a toaster made from welding wire.*

Glaswegians often glimpsed into the yards from the top deck of the trams, but usually didn't get a view like this. This is Fairfield's, with the Empress of Japan *about to receive attention in one of the most famous and busiest yards in the world.*

30

The sheer scale of manufacturing in shipyards could be awesome. Here the workers are almost dwarfed by one of the gigantic propellers being fitted to the QE2 at John Brown in Clydebank.

34

In winter, when darkness fell, work often continued on the floodlit vessels – a spectacular sight. This giant gas carrier is shown nearing completion in the Kvaerner yard, which took over Govan Shipbuilders in 1988.

It is only when you see the individual sections of a liner under construction that the size and complexity can be fully appreciated. Workers cling to rather rickety-looking scaffolding as the top of the funnel of the Transvaal Castle *is lowered into position in Browns.*

It was the beginning of an era for The Transvaal Castle, *but for the* Captain Cook *this is the start of its last voyage, tugs straining to take it down river to the open sea in 1959. A famous emigrant ship, the* Cook *transported thousands of Scots to new lives on the other side of the world.*

40

The shipyard workers were as tough as the ships they built. Inevitably there were industrial disputes. Even during the Second World War there were 'token' strikes. These grim-faced workers are leaving the yard on one such occasion.

This evocative shot shows the grim reality of the mass meeting. It is 1965 and in Fairfield an official of the Amalgamated Engineering Union addresses the workers in the engine shop. The conflicts at such meetings and disputes spawned a host of brilliant orators.

42

Welder, plumber, plater, shipwright . . . four of the trades that helped create the great ships of the world, and four of the faces of the men who plied their trades in Lithgow's, in Port Glasgow, in the '60s.

A new great 'Queen' and a tight piece of manoeuvering reminiscent of the classic image of the Queen Mary *on the cover as the* QE2 *is inched into Greenock dry dock in 1968. Horsepower moves the elegant giant around the world's oceans but here some good old-fashioned manpower is required.*

46

Nowadays a nautical traffic jam on the river is a rarity, but here there is not much room to spare as Uganda, *under tow, heads up river past the most famous vessel left on the Clyde, the sea-going paddler* Waverley, *the last of her kind in the world.*

50

The three great 'Queens', the Cunarders, *are legendary for their beauty, but for some Clydesiders the most attractive of liners were the* Empress *ships. This is the third* Empress of Britain *leaving the Clyde in 1956 on an exceptionally high tide.*

The yards were not an entirely male environment. Mrs Mary Scott was a woman who looked well able to hold her own in a man's world. This is the '50s and she is the 'rivet catcher'. The 'rivet heater' throws the rivet from the furnace to be caught by the catcher's tongs.

A head for heights was a must for most yard workers.
Not much time for the fine view of the river,
neighbouring yards or the rolling hills beyond, as the
upper decks of the Sylvania are plated.

The Clydebank yard workers and their families suffered dreadfully in the Blitz. This is one of the most evocative images from that tragic time as bombed out Bankies wander the blitzed streets. In two nights of bombing in 1941, 1200 Clydesiders died – more than 500 from Clydebank alone.

The horrors of the war were a distant, if not forgotten, memory for these sunbathers on the front at Helensburgh in the '50s. The new electric 'blue trains' from Glasgow whisked day-trippers down the coast for a paddle or a dip in the pool.

A fine image of the mixture of rural and industrial landscapes that is such a feature of the Clyde. Church spires mingle with factory chimneys in this view looking back up river over Greenock and Port Glasgow.

An early evening photograph capturing Gourock's dominant situation on the Clyde, with the hills of Argyll in the background. The occasion was a Royal visit in the '60s, and the flotilla is composed of assorted naval vessels, including submarines.

Across the Firth in Dunoon the Cowal games attract huge crowds each summer – though it is said they also attract more than their fair share of rain. The Highland dancing is a major attraction and this young performer is taking it very seriously.

Sweet Rothesay bay is a favourite of Glaswegians to this day. This aerial
picture shows the castle to good effect as shipping comes and goes in a
busy harbour with the *Royal Yacht Britannia* lying at anchor off shore.

The Clyde's beaches these days are busy with folk in trainers and anoraks. Life on Largs foreshore in the early part of the century was a tad more formal. Jackets, collars, ties, hats, raincoat over the arm and even a walking stick feature in this shot.

Later in the '30s, the attire was still formal, even when cooling the feet with a nice little paddle. Why you need an umbrella and a hat for this pleasant pursuit is not clear!

These days, when huge outdoor pools can lie derelict, it is an eye-opener to see the pulling-power of pools in the '30s. Galas were common, with comedy diving acts and swimming races. This is Prestwick on a summer Saturday in 1935.

Yachting in the Firth is a passion for many Clydesiders. If you can afford it, you sail; if you can't, you watch. Yacht-spotters young and old are knowledgeable about the comings and goings of famous craft. This is Drum *in a stiff breeze. Once owned by pop star Simon le Bon, it is now a familiar sight on the Clyde.*

74

Dunoon pier on a summer day, with the Queen Mary II *alongside. You can almost smell the hot oil from the engines and home baking from the tea room, an evocative picture of the way it was in the heyday of holidays 'doon the watter'.*

There is no guarantee of sun on the Costa Clyde – rain hats, windbreaks and plastic coats are a must. This little fellow is as well oilskinned as a Newfoundland fisherman and as proud of the fish he has caught as he would be of a giant cod.

Holiday snaps, as the little fisherman showed, are vital for reviving the memories during dark winter nights. The young chap in the centre of this picture is delighted with his souvenir. In contrast, the young lady on the left has an apprehensive air.

A lasting memory of the Glasgow Fair was the trek down from the train to the pier at Wemyss Bay for the Rothesay ferry. Laughter, good humour and the expectation of a happy holiday as the passengers' footsteps echo around the wooden walkway.

Once across the Firth at the Fair, there was little chance of escaping the crowds. The Duchess of Montrose, *one of the most elegant of Clyde steamers, has disembarked this huge crowd of holidaymakers heading ashore for their 'digs' in Rothesay.*

84

Another stylish vessel was the King Edward. *Here it makes a stop on a trip round the Kyles of Bute. The happy holidaymakers seem to be enjoying a paddle despite the proximity of a waste pipe – simpler days in a world without EU directives!*

In the Mediterranean resorts Scots are famous for their reckless attitude to sunbathing. Ironically, back at home in the '50s, this group shows a more cautious approach. But it is not designer fashion – not a logo in sight. Hats made from newspapers and handkerchiefs, and boots instead of trainers.

Some Ayrshire beaches these days are deserted, but at Barassie in 1967, just around the corner from Troon, you were a wimp if you didn't drive right on to the sand. And neither the cold nor the quality of the water kept you from a swim.

One of the delights of a sail down the Clyde was the ship's band. Requests were a speciality and the bands helped add to the fun, especially on the longer trips such as Gourock to Campbeltown.

Striking sunsets are a feature of the west coast and even industrial landmarks can adopt a certain elegance, as shown here by the twin cranes of Hunterston Ore Terminal near Largs.

It is often the simplest of pleasures that make the memories. Here some youngsters enjoy a spot of fishing at Corrie pier. No doubt they also went on more exotic holidays and adventures in Spain and Florida, but they are unlikely ever to forget their days on Arran.

Sailing into history. There is now talk of new fast ferries criss-crossing the Firth, but the great days of the Clyde steamers are over – only the Waverley remains as a reminder of a proud past. New-style holidaymakers are now going down the Clyde – yachtsmen, golfers and walkers. Times have changed but the beauty lingers on.